D1121362

Large as Life

This edition first published in 2004
(originally published in hardback, 2000)
by Miles Kelly Publishing Ltd
Bardfield Centre, Great Bardfield, Essex, CM7 4SL

2 4 6 8 10 9 7 5 3 1

British Library Cataloguing-in-Publication Data
A catalogue record for this book is available from the British library

ISBN 1-84236-455-3

Printed in China

Editorial Director: Belinda Gallagher
Designer: Sarah Ponder
Cover Designer: Jo Brewer
Production Manager: Estela Boulton
Indexer: Jane Parker

www.mileskelly.net
info@mileskelly.net

Large as Life

Illustrated by Alan Male
Written by Steve Parker

Miles Kelly
PUBLISHING

Contents

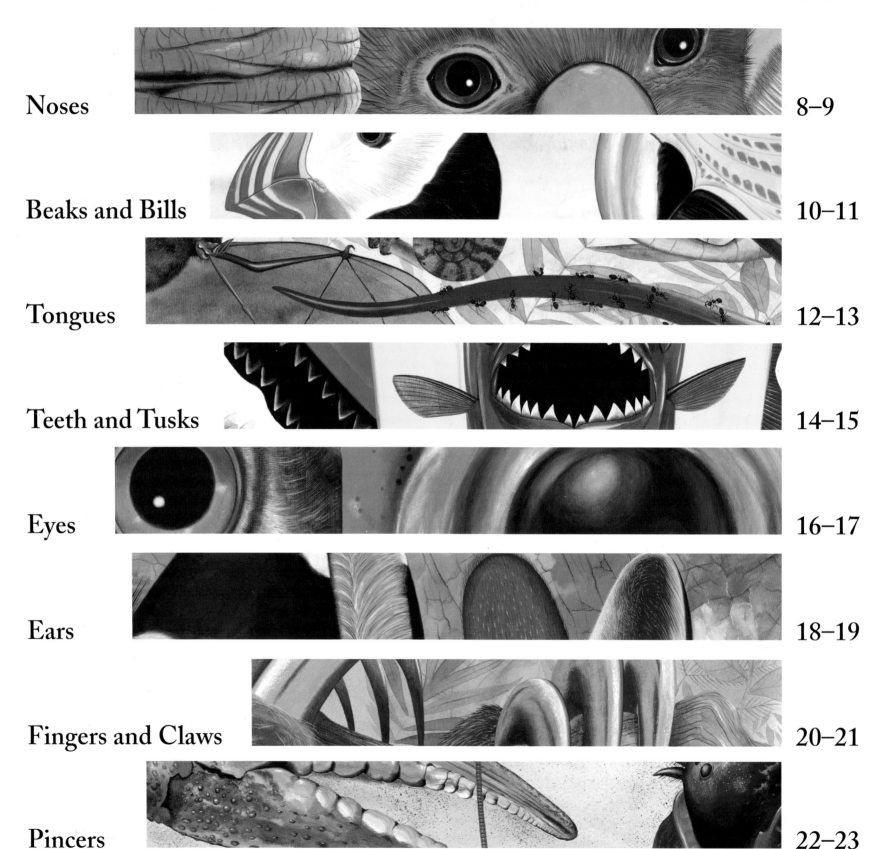

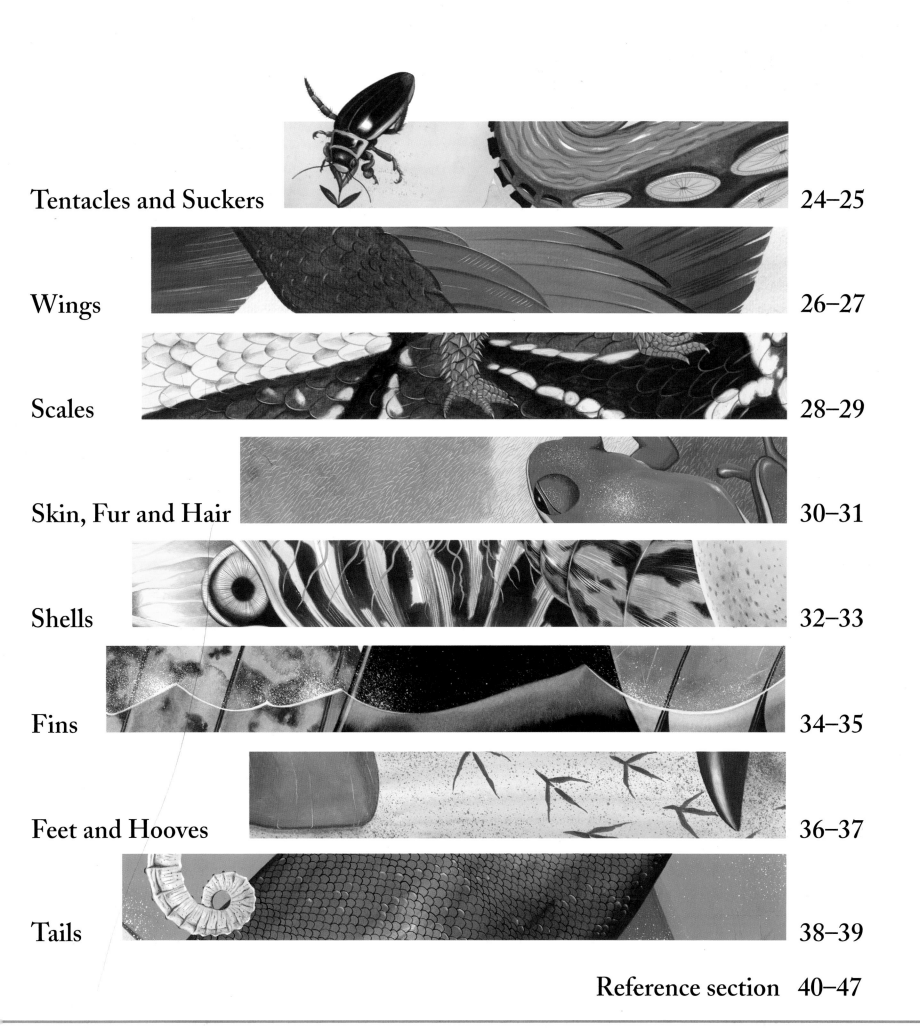

That's
about
the size of it

This is a book about the sizes of animals. It should have a picture of the world's biggest creature – the blue whale. But it cannot. At least, not a whole blue whale. That would cover an area the size of 3,000 pages, because every animal in this book is shown real size, actual size, same size – *as large as life*. Since each page is considerably smaller than a tennis court, we can only show bits and pieces of bigger beasts. But there are plenty of whole smaller animals, down to hummingbirds, newts, caterpillars and flies.

Never before has a book shown the kingdom of creatures in such a life-like and immediate way. It's the next best thing to a zoo at your elbow. If you want to compare your fingers with those of the aye-aye, your feet with a crocodile's, and your skin with that of a naked mole rat – simply place them on the page. For some body parts you might need a mirror!

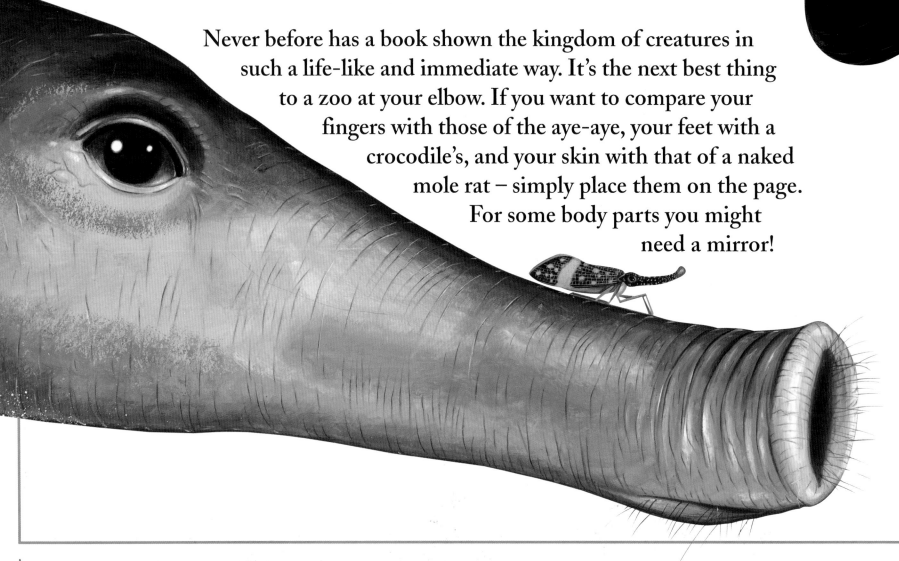

The book starts at the beginning with a batch of noses. It finishes at the end with a swish of tails. In between are eyes, ears, tongues, teeth, legs, feet, wings, fins, suckers, shells, scales and many other body parts. Each creature has been chosen for a special reason. Some are adapted in intricate ways to their environments. Others have amazing design features that are unique in the animal kingdom.

The creatures shown come from every habitat around the world, from tropics to poles. They come from all major animal groups, from worms to whales. The reference section at the end gives essential details about each type or species, where it lives and what it eats.

So turn the pages, look with wonder, compare with awe, and see how you measure up!

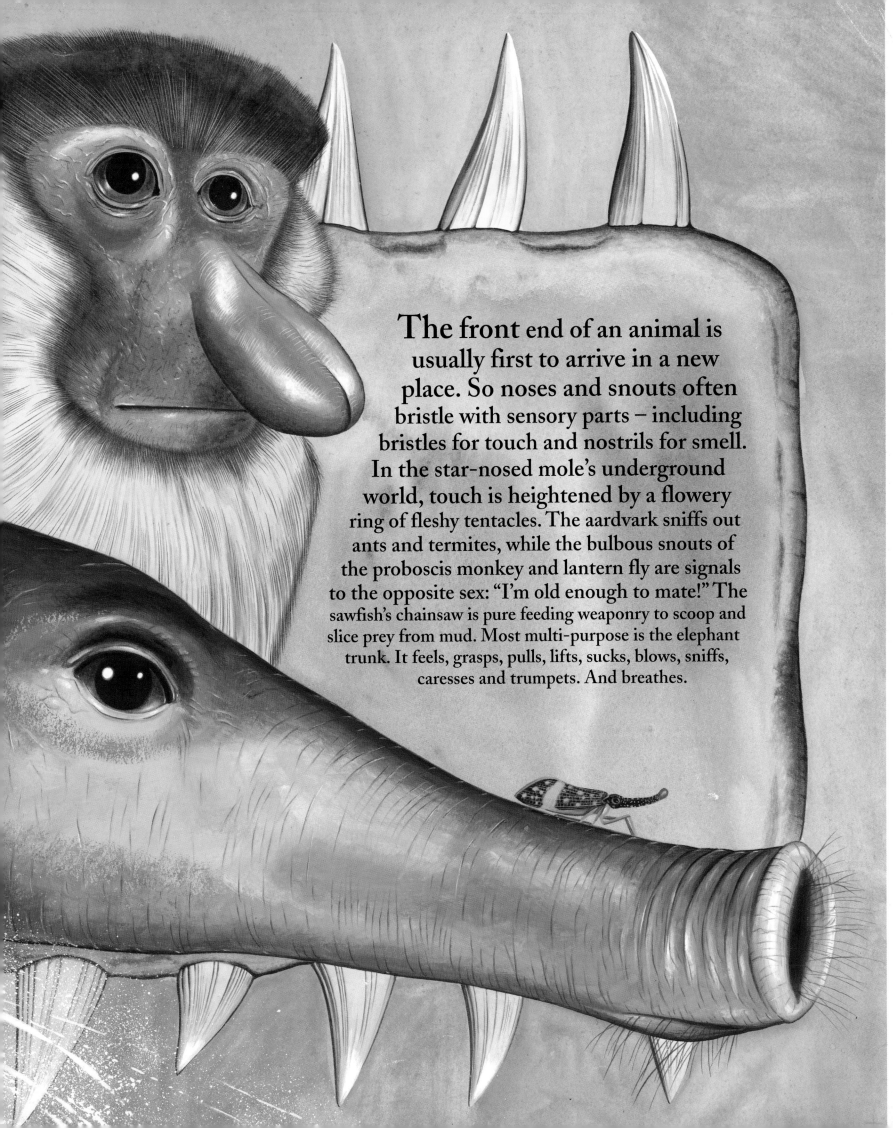

The front end of an animal is usually first to arrive in a new place. So noses and snouts often bristle with sensory parts – including bristles for touch and nostrils for smell. In the star-nosed mole's underground world, touch is heightened by a flowery ring of fleshy tentacles. The aardvark sniffs out ants and termites, while the bulbous snouts of the proboscis monkey and lantern fly are signals to the opposite sex: "I'm old enough to mate!" The sawfish's chainsaw is pure feeding weaponry to scoop and slice prey from mud. Most multi-purpose is the elephant trunk. It feels, grasps, pulls, lifts, sucks, blows, sniffs, caresses and trumpets. And breathes.

Star-nosed mole
Nose tentacles 3 cm across

Asian elephant
Trunk up to 2 m long

Koala
Nose 8 cm long

Aardvark
Snout 20 cm long

Proboscis monkey
Nose 6 cm long (male only)

Sawfish
Saw-edged snout 2 m long

Lantern fly
Bulging snout up to 3 cm long

Like tools of the trade,
beaks and bills vary in shape
according to the jobs they tackle.
The long, thin, curved pliers of the
sicklebill reach into flowers for nectar. The
high-pressure boltcutters of the macaw split
even the hardest nuts. The sharp spear of the
pelican is ideal for impaling fish. Beaks are visual
symbols too. The colourful puffin's bill becomes even
brighter in season to show the owner is ready to
breed. Not only birds have beak-like mouths. The
platypus dabbles in stream-bed mud for worms
and shellfish. The alligator snapping turtle's beaky,
sharp-edged mouth could cut a fish
in two – or your finger.

White-tipped sicklebill
Bill 4 cm long

Platypus
Bill 10 cm long

Atlantic puffin
Beak 4.5 cm long

Alligator snapping turtle
Mouth 10 cm wide

Brown kiwi
Beak up to 20 cm

Brown pelican
Bill up to 50 cm

Scarlet macaw
Beak 10 cm around curve

11

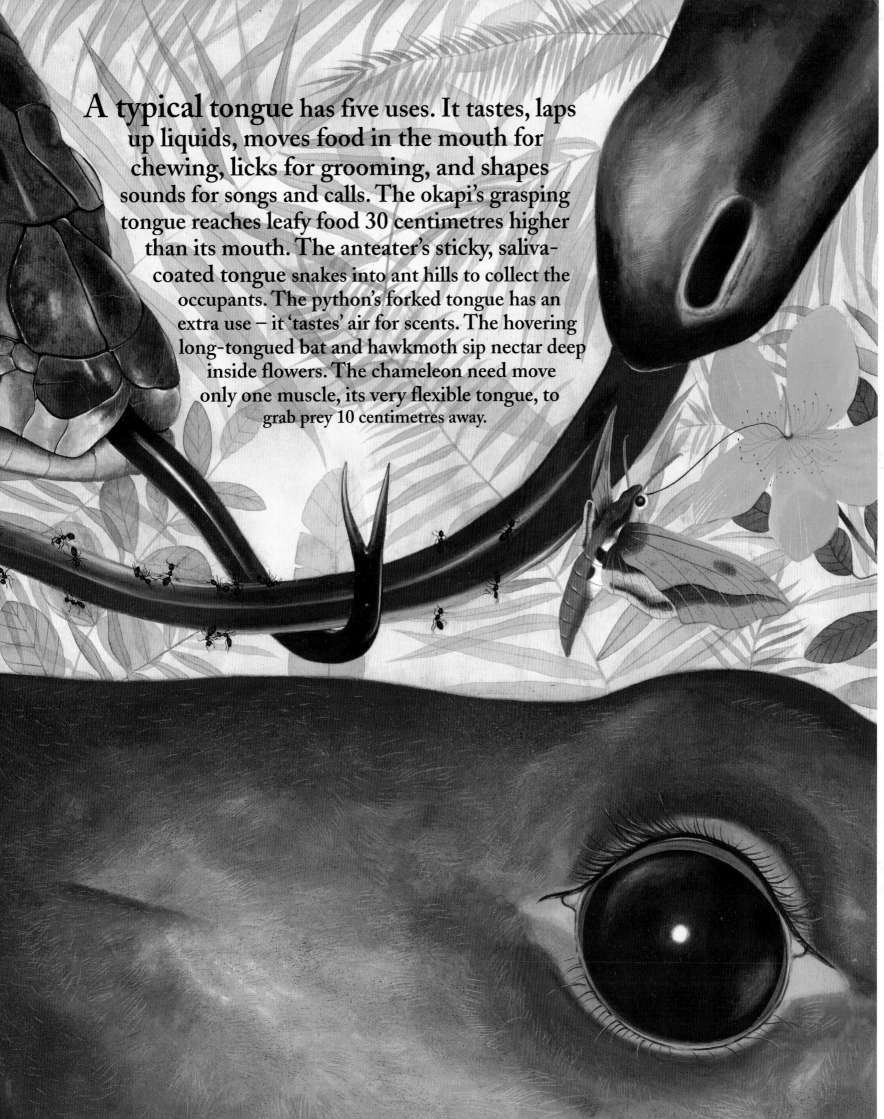

A typical tongue has five uses. It tastes, laps up liquids, moves food in the mouth for chewing, licks for grooming, and shapes sounds for songs and calls. The okapi's grasping tongue reaches leafy food 30 centimetres higher than its mouth. The anteater's sticky, saliva-coated tongue snakes into ant hills to collect the occupants. The python's forked tongue has an extra use – it 'tastes' air for scents. The hovering long-tongued bat and hawkmoth sip nectar deep inside flowers. The chameleon need move only one muscle, its very flexible tongue, to grab prey 10 centimetres away.

Flap-necked chameleon
Tongue 12 cm maximum

Indian python
Tongue 15 cm

Giant anteater
Tongue up to 60 cm

Long-tongued bat
Tongue 3 cm

Darwin's hawk moth
Proboscis 4 cm

Okapi
Tongue 30 cm

13

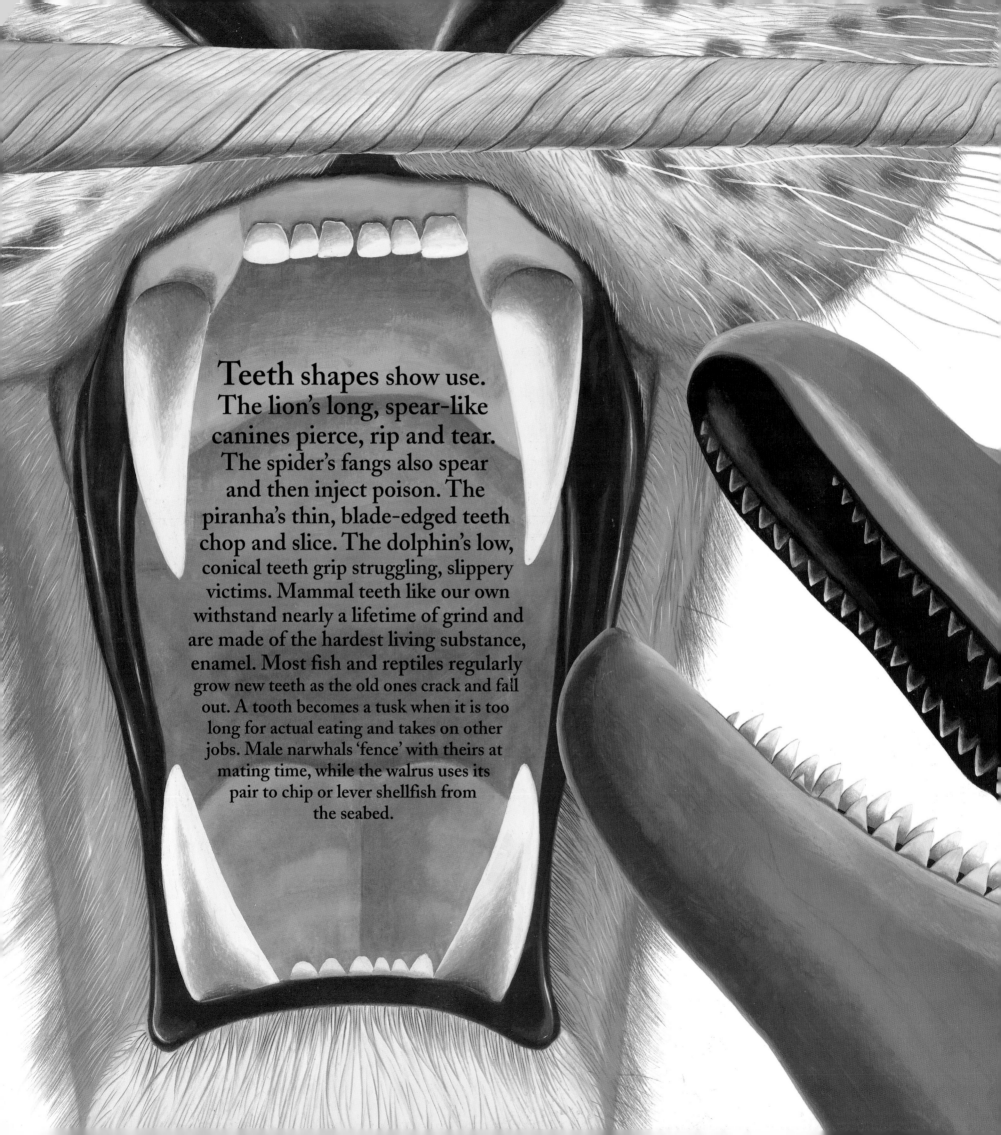

Teeth shapes show use. The lion's long, spear-like canines pierce, rip and tear. The spider's fangs also spear and then inject poison. The piranha's thin, blade-edged teeth chop and slice. The dolphin's low, conical teeth grip struggling, slippery victims. Mammal teeth like our own withstand nearly a lifetime of grind and are made of the hardest living substance, enamel. Most fish and reptiles regularly grow new teeth as the old ones crack and fall out. A tooth becomes a tusk when it is too long for actual eating and takes on other jobs. Male narwhals 'fence' with theirs at mating time, while the walrus uses its pair to chip or lever shellfish from the seabed.

Narwhal
*Tusk up to 2.6 m
long (male only)*

Lion
*Canine teeth
8 cm long*

**Bottle-nosed
dolphin**
*Teeth up to
12 mm long*

Walrus
Tusk 60 cm long

Red piranha
*Teeth up to
10 mm long*

**Bird-eating
spider**
*Fangs up to
12 mm*

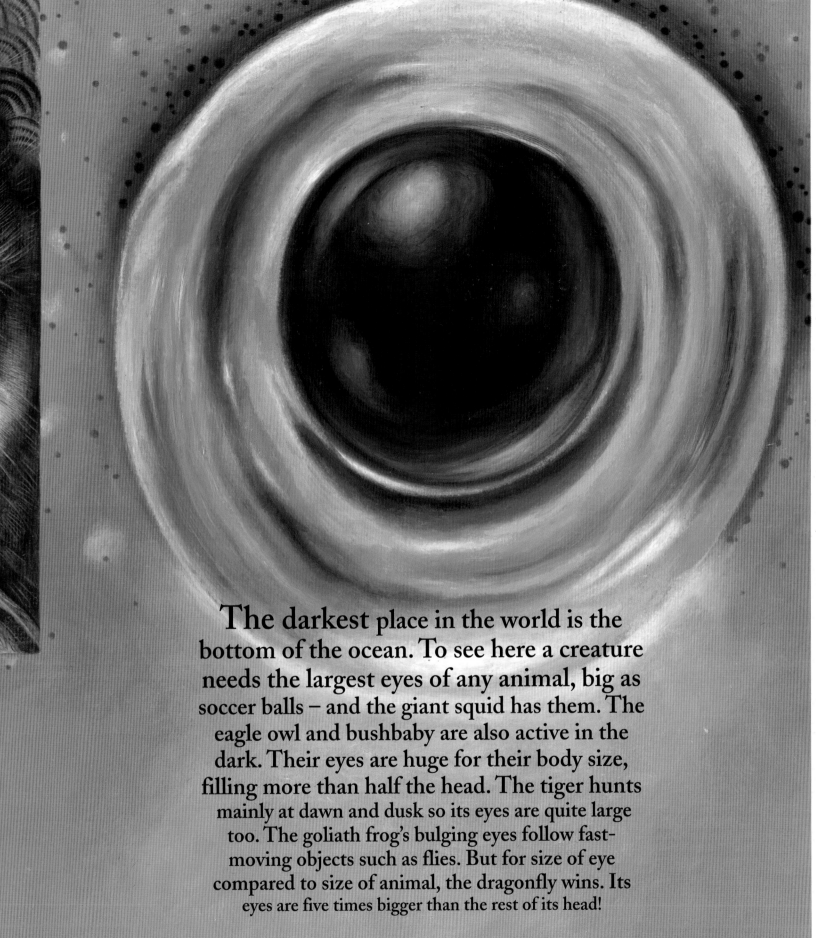

The darkest place in the world is the bottom of the ocean. To see here a creature needs the largest eyes of any animal, big as soccer balls – and the giant squid has them. The eagle owl and bushbaby are also active in the dark. Their eyes are huge for their body size, filling more than half the head. The tiger hunts mainly at dawn and dusk so its eyes are quite large too. The goliath frog's bulging eyes follow fast-moving objects such as flies. But for size of eye compared to size of animal, the dragonfly wins. Its eyes are five times bigger than the rest of its head!

Bengal tiger
Eye 3.5 cm across

Giant squid
Eye up to 40 cm across

Goliath frog
Eye up to 3 cm across

Verraux's eagle owl
Eye 5 cm across

Ruddy dragonfly
Eye up to 4 mm across

Lesser bushbaby
Eye 2 cm across

Sssshhhhhh ... ears pick up the slightest sounds. Big is best for collecting sound waves. A rustle in the grass alerts the zebra to danger. Some ears detect a narrow range of sounds. The toad hears little else except its kind's mating calls. Some ears are not even on the head – the cricket's are on its knees! Ears have other uses besides just hearing. One is finding the way. The bat detects echoes of its own squeaks and so flies in the dark by echolocation. Another use is temperature control. In scorching heat the jackrabbit, fennec fox and flapping elephant ears lose excess body heat to keep the owner cool.

Grevy's zebra
Ear 25 cm long

Slit-faced bat
Ear flap 4 cm long

Bush cricket
Ear membrane 1 mm across

African elephant
Ear flap up to 1.5 m wide

Black-tailed jackrabbit
Ear 20 cm long

Cane toad
Ear drum 17 mm across

Fennec fox
Ear 15 cm long

19

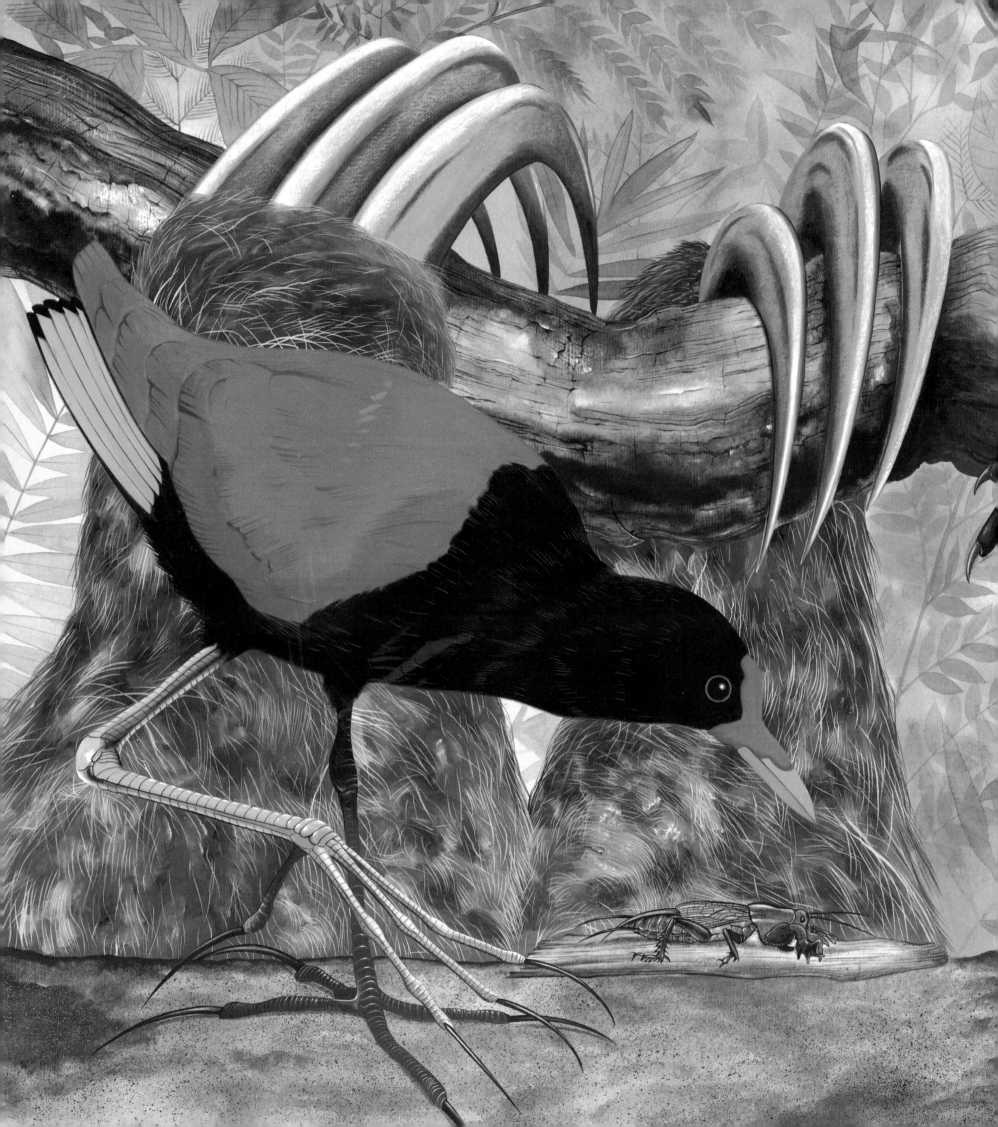

You probably use your fingers to write with a pen, type at a keyboard, count on a calculator – and poke into all kinds of places! Animals poke about too, usually for food or shelter or safety. The aye-aye (a type of lemur) pokes its meal of grubs from under bark and stones. However most other creatures have claws, not nails. These are tree hooks for the sloth and bear, and soil shovels for the mole and mole cricket. The barn owl grips perches and grabs prey with its fearsome talons. The same parts in the jacana are long and light to tiptoe over floating leaves.

Sun bear
Longest claws 7 cm long

European mole
Forelimb claws 8–12 mm long

Three-toed sloth
Claw 10 cm around curve

Aye-aye
Middle finger 12–15 cm long

Barn owl
Talons 2 cm long

American jacana (lilytrotter)
Longest toes 10 cm long

Mole cricket
Digging forelimb 2 cm long

21

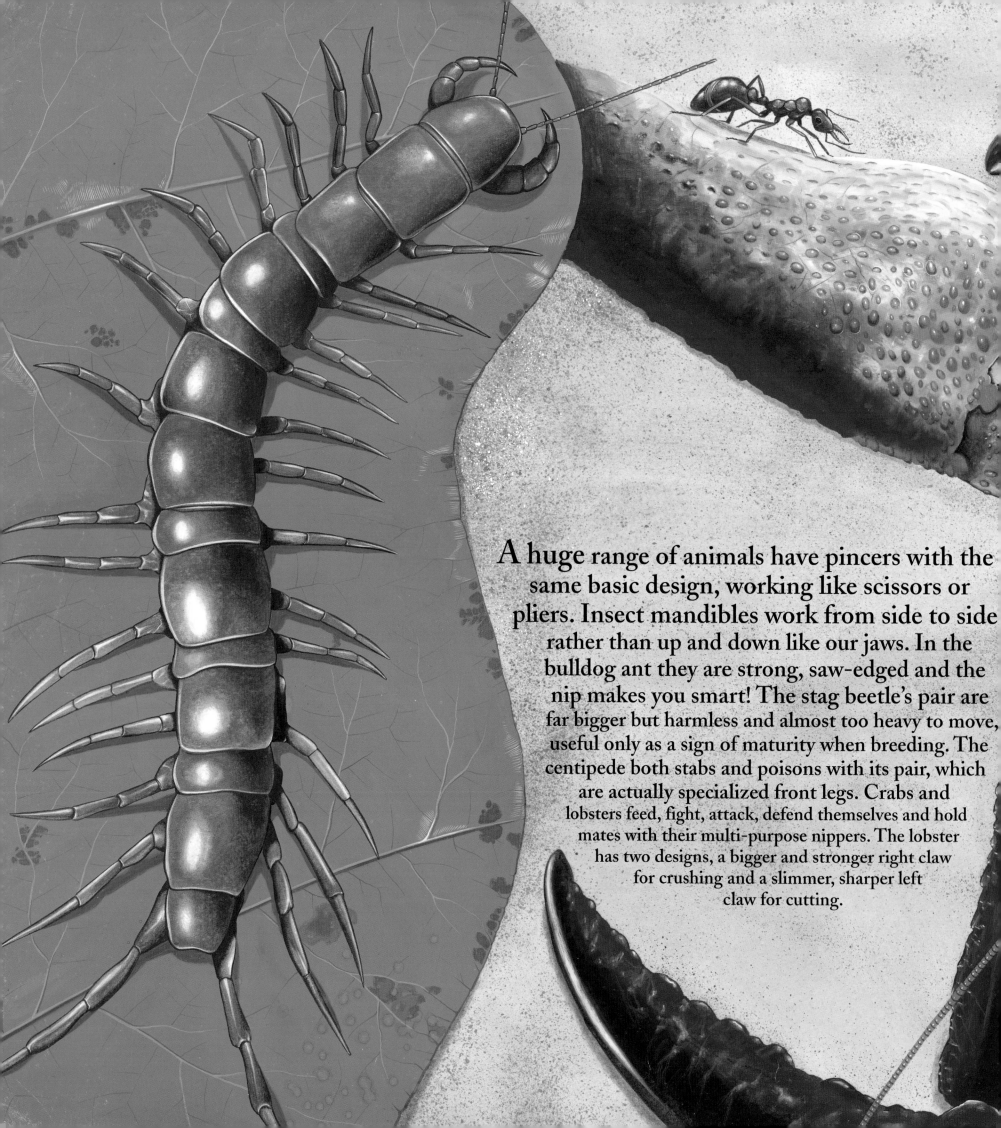

A huge range of animals have pincers with the same basic design, working like scissors or pliers. Insect mandibles work from side to side rather than up and down like our jaws. In the bulldog ant they are strong, saw-edged and the nip makes you smart! The stag beetle's pair are far bigger but harmless and almost too heavy to move, useful only as a sign of maturity when breeding. The centipede both stabs and poisons with its pair, which are actually specialized front legs. Crabs and lobsters feed, fight, attack, defend themselves and hold mates with their multi-purpose nippers. The lobster has two designs, a bigger and stronger right claw for crushing and a slimmer, sharper left claw for cutting.

Giant (Japanese) spider crab
Pincer claws up to 20 cm long

North Atlantic lobster
Larger pincer claw up to 30 cm long

Giant centipede
Fang-pincers 25 mm long

Bulldog ant
Mandibles 7–8 mm long

Stag beetle
Antler-like mandibles 2 cm long (male only)

Our own arms and legs can bend, but only at certain places. The idea of a totally flexible tentacle is very strange. Having more than four limbs is stranger still. Yet the octopus has eight, the humble anemone may have more than 50 tentacles and the jellyfish trails several hundred! Suckers are useful to the octopus for feeding; to the leech for moving; and to the male diving beetle for mating. He uses his tiny foreleg suckers only at breeding time to cling to his partner. Suckers can also just suck. The remora sticks to a shark by the sucker on top of its head which resembles the sole of a training shoe!

Great diving beetle
Foreleg sucker 3 mm across (male only)

Giant Pacific octopus
Tentacle (arm) 1.5 m long, suckers up to 10 cm across

Snakelocks sea anemone
Tentacles about 10 cm long

Lion's mane jellyfish
Longest tentacles exceed 10 m

Medicinal leech
15 cm at full stretch, suckers up to 20 mm across

Remora (sharksucker)
Sucker 15 cm long

25

Up, up and away! Only three groups of animals truly master the air – birds, bats and insects. Wing shapes show flying styles. Long, broad wings soar as the condor rides the mountain's rising winds for hours without a flap. Shorter, more pointed wings allow the bee-eater to twist and turn after insect prey. If that insect is a cockchafer it stands little chance of escape since it is a noisy, clumsy flier. Moths flutter to display their beautiful wings for possible mates. Champion gliding mammal is the colugo, a tropical forest relative of shrews and moles. The flying fish swims fast, leaps above the water and glides away from enemies on wing-like fins.

Bee-eater
Wing span 30 cm

**Colugo
(flying lemur)**
*Skinflap span
up to 70 cm*

Cockchafer
Wing span 9 cm

**Giant moon
moth**
Wing span 20 cm

**Andean
condor**
*Wing span may
exceed 2.5 m*

**Two-finned
flying fish**
*Wing span
30 cm*

Only fish, reptiles and birds (on their legs) have true scales. The huge sturgeon and the pinecone fish have large, rigid scales. So does the armadillo lizard, and its scales have sharp points too. In all these creatures the scales are mainly for protection. But they limit the body's bending and movements. The scales on snakes like the viper, and on the legs of birds such as the non-flying cassowary, are smaller and thinner. This allows more bending and easier movement. The sharp-edged 'scales' on the pangolin, an ant-eating mammal, are really hard plates made of horn (a substance like our fingernails).

Gaboon viper
Belly scales up to 10 mm wide

Giant pangolin
Scales up to 5 cm wide

Cassowary
Leg and foot scales up to 2.5 cm wide

Sturgeon
Large side scales (scutes) up to 10 cm wide

Pinecone fish
Scales 1 cm wide

Armadillo lizard
Scales 5–10 mm wide

Your fur is most obvious on your head. It's on your body too, though shorter and thinner than on most mammals so your skin shows through. Some mammals have even less fur, like the rhino and that strange underground creature from Africa, the naked mole rat. Colour and pattern are vital for wild animals. A giraffe's patches conceal its tall body in the dappled shade of trees. The green tree frog matches its leafy home. The black panther cannot change its spots – it's a very dark version of the leopard that occurs as part of natural variation. Don't cuddle the woolly bear caterpillar either. Its hairs snap to release stinging fluid as self defence.

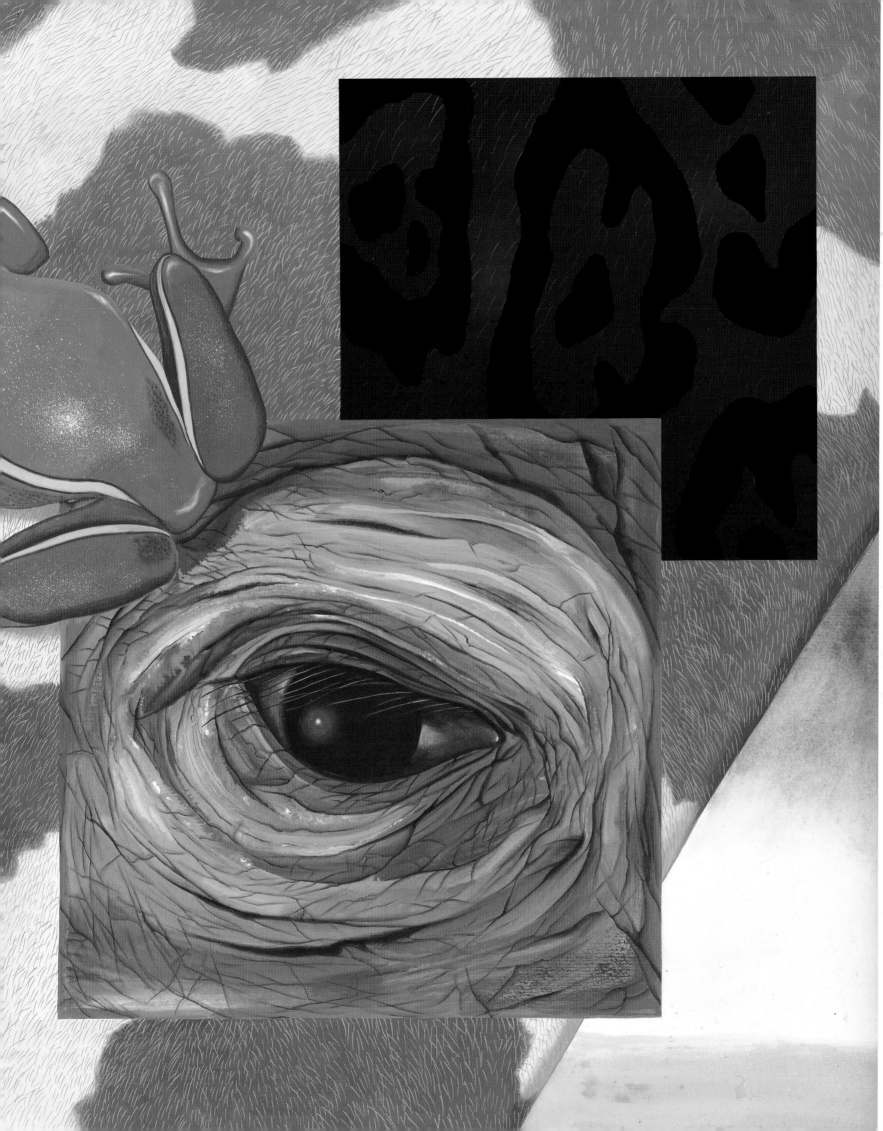

Giraffe
Hairs 3-5 cm long

**Black panther
(leopard)**
*Rosette 'spots' up
to 10 cm across*

**Green tree
frog**
*Up to 5,000
poison glands
in skin*

**Naked mole
rat**
*Sparse hairs
up to 2 cm long*

**White
(square-lipped)
rhinoceros**
*Skin up to 3 cm
thick*

**Woolly bear
caterpillar**
*Hairs up to
6 cm long*

31

Shells

are to hide in, especially for animals in the mollusc group. The giant African snail withdraws completely into its hard home. In the ocean, the glorious starshell is a tiny and delicate sea-living snail. The file shell flaps its two shell halves to swim jerkily. The nautilus, another mollusc, is a shelled cousin of the octopus and a similarly fierce predator. Goose barnacles look like molluscs but they are crustacean, cousins of crabs. Shells are also to hatch from. The biggest shelled egg is laid by the ostrich. But it is dwarfed by the largest shell of all, which is simply for protection and covers the back of the giant tortoise.

Glorious starshell
Main shell 2 cm, spikes up to 1 cm

File shell
Shell 10 cm long

Goose barnacle
Shell 5 cm long

Ostrich (egg)
Whole egg 16 x 14 cm

Nautilus
Shell 30 cm across

Giant African land snail
Shell 25 cm long

Galapagos giant tortoise
Shell up to 1 m long

Like wings in air, fins in water propel and control. They let their owners push forwards, rise or dive, steer and turn, brake to a sudden stop, and of course swim in a straight line. Dorsal fins are on the back or upper surface, as on the killer whale (the largest type of dolphin), sailfish and shark. They prevent the animal spinning like a corkscrew as it swims. The cuttlefish ripples its lateral fin to stay perfectly steady in the water. The lionfish wafts its fins lazily, its gaudy colours warning of the deadly poison in its fin spines. Like most body parts, fins can show their owner's readiness to breed, as in the newt's crest.

Killer whale (orca)
Male's dorsal fin 2 m tall

Great white shark
Main dorsal fin 70 cm tall

Sailfish
Fin 65 cm tall, 1.5 m long

Cuttlefish
Body fin up to 5 cm wide

Lionfish (scorpionfish)
Fin spines up to 25 cm long

Great crested newt
Fin or crest 10 mm tall

35

Most feet are for walking – or running, leaping, climbing and tiptoeing. Wide, smooth-based feet spread body weight so the animal does not sink in soft ground, like the camel in desert sand. Long toes do the same as the flamingo wades in soft mud. Lobed or webbed toes help to increase foot area for pushing water, which is how the coot and crocodile swim. Other feet and toes are just the opposite – designed with rough, non-slip soles. This allows the gecko to cling upside down to ceilings and the penguin to stand and walk safely on the slippery Antarctic ice.

Emperor penguin
Foot 12 cm wide

Tokay gecko
Footspan 2.5 cm

Dromedary camel
Foot 25 cm wide

Greater flamingo
Longest toes 15 cm

Nile crocodile
Foot 30 cm long

Coot
Foot up to 15 cm long, up to 12 cm wide

We lack tails, so it's difficult to imagine their huge variety of uses. The spider monkey's is so mobile and prehensile (grasping) it's almost like having another arm and hand. The seahorse clings with its curly tail since it is a poor swimmer. The dolphin, on the other hand, could go nowhere without its flukes. The scorpion's tail bears a deadly sting for both hunting and self-defence. The beaver slaps its flat tail loudly on to the water, to warn others in its family of danger. The lemur holds its tail in different positions to show its moods to other members of its group. Finally the woodwasp's tail looks most dangerous. But it is a harmless hollow tube for drilling into wood and laying eggs.

Humpback dolphin
Tail flukes 60 cm across

American beaver
Tail 25 cm long

Giant woodwasp
'Sting' (ovipositor) 2 cm

Imperial scorpion
Tail 9 cm around curve including sting

Seahorse
Tail 10 cm when straight

Ring-tailed lemur
Tail 55 cm long

Black spider monkey
Tail 70 cm when straight

39

Animal profiles

In this section of the book you can find every animal that has been featured on earlier pages. These animals have been shrunk down to 'normal' book size, to fit in the whole creature. There is information on where each animal is found, what it eats, and fascinating snippets about its daily life.

INSECTS

Giant moon moth (p27)
Argema (various types)
• SIZE Body and tail up to 20 cm
• SIZE OF WINGS Span 20 cm
• RANGE Africa
• HABITAT Woods
• FOOD Leaves of various trees such as marula and eugenia
Among the world's largest moths, moon moths are named after their moon-like wing markings. The male's feathery antennae (feelers) pick up the scent of a female from 2–3 km away.

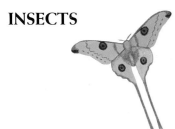

Great diving beetle (p25)
Dytiscus marginalis
• SIZE Total length 4–5 cm
• SIZE OF SUCKER ON FRONT LEG 3 mm
• RANGE Europe
• HABITAT Ponds, streams
• FOOD Tadpoles, fish fry and similar small water animals
The male holds the female with the suckers near the end of his front legs while mating. He may also attach himself to an underwater stem or twig with them. These beetles surface for fresh air every few minutes.

Mole cricket (p21)
Gryllotalpa (various types)
• SIZE Total length 6 cm
• SIZE OF DIGGING 'FOOT' (FRONT LEG) 2 cm
• RANGE Most regions worldwide
• HABITAT Woods, bush, plains
• FOOD Bits and pieces of plants and animals
The strong, hard forelimbs of the mole cricket scrape and dig out its tunnel home, where it rests and also partly feeds. The male's burrow has a tapering shape almost like a loudspeaker to louden his mating chirp.

40

Lantern fly (lantern bug) (p9)
Lanternaria (hundreds of kinds)
• SIZE Total length up to 10 cm (in some tropical kinds)
• SIZE OF NOSE Up to 3 cm
• RANGE Worldwide – except cold regions
• HABITAT Woods, scrub, grassland
• FOOD Plant juices
Some lantern flies have snouts longer than their bodies! The enormous front end is designed to attract a mate and is mostly hollow so the bug flies rather than nose-dives. Sadly, this insect is misnamed – its nose looks as though it might glow, but doesn't.

Stag beetle (p23)
Lucanus cervus
• SIZE Total length 7 cm
• SIZE OF MANDIBLES 2 cm
• RANGE Europe, west Asia
• HABITAT Woods, meadows, hedges, bush
• FOOD Grubs (larvae) eat old wood, especially oak; adults do not eat
The male's antler-like mandibles (jawed mouthparts) are so big and clumsy they cannot bite. But they can grip a rival male for contests at breeding time. The female's mandibles are much smaller and give a strong nip.

Cockchafer (p27)
Melolontha and various other types
• SIZE Head and body up to 4 cm
• SIZE OF WINGS Span 9 cm
• RANGE Worldwide in warmer regions
• HABITAT Woods, bush
• FOOD Leaves and other plant parts
Cockchafer beetles are also called May or June bugs. This is when the adults emerge from the soil after 2–3 years there as grubs, eating plant roots. The adults buzz noisily and seem suicidal as they crash clumsily into windows.

Bulldog ant (p23)
Myrmecia (many types)
• SIZE Head and body up to 4 cm
• SIZE OF MANDIBLES 7–8 mm
• RANGE Australia and Southeast Asia
• HABITAT Forests
• FOOD Adults eat mainly flower nectar; grubs are fed mashed-up worms, termites and other small creatures
Some ants give an uncomfortable nip, but you really know about the jabbing pain from a bulldog ant bite. The fearsome saw-edged pincers are the main jaw-like mouthparts called mandibles.

Ruddy dragonfly (p17)
Sympetrum sanguineum
• SIZE Head and body 5 cm
• SIZE OF EYE 4 mm
• RANGE Lakes, rivers, marshes
• HABITAT Europe, North Africa, Middle East
• FOOD Small flying insects
Darter dragonflies, like the ruddy sympetrum, tend to watch from a perch for passing prey and then dart out to catch it, rather than patrol on the wing like other dragonflies. They (along with the mantises) have the biggest eyes of any insect.

Bush cricket (p19)
Tettigonia (various types)
• SIZE Head and body 6 cm
• SIZE OF EAR MEMBRANE Width 1 mm
• RANGE Most warm regions worldwide
• HABITAT Woods, scrub, bush
• FOOD Vegetation
Crickets have ears on their back pair of knees! The long, flexible antennae detect touch, scents and air currents such as winds, as well as certain sounds. Only the male chirps, to attract a female at breeding time.

Giant woodwasp (p39)
Uroceras (various types)
• SIZE Head and body 3–4 cm
• SIZE OF TAIL Up to 2 cm
• RANGE Most temperate regions
• HABITAT Forests, woods
• FOOD Grubs (larvae) eat wood
The frightening-looking 'sting' of a female woodwasp is in fact a harmless ovipositor – a tube through which she lays her eggs. She pushes it through the bark of a tree into the sapwood and then lays up to 400 eggs.

Darwin's hawk moth (p13)
Xanthopan morgani
• SIZE Head and body length 5 cm
• SIZE OF TONGUE 4 cm
• RANGE Southeast Asia, Australia
• HABITAT Woods, forests
• FOOD Nectar
The 'tongue' of a butterfly or moth is actually its tube-shaped proboscis. It coils under the head like a spiral spring, then straightens out like a drinking-straw to sip sweet flower nectar.

OTHER INVERTEBRATES

Woolly bear caterpillar (p31)
Hundreds of kinds
• SIZE Up to 10 cm long
• SIZE OF HAIRS Up to 6 cm long
• RANGE Worldwide
• HABITAT Woods, shrubland, grassland
• FOOD Leaves
Many kinds of butterflies and moths have hairy caterpillars. Usually the hairs are brittle and hollow. They snap easily to release irritating or stinging chemicals as a form of defence against predators such as birds.

Giant African land snail (p33)
Acatina (several types)
• SIZE Total length 35 cm (at full stretch)
• SIZE OF SHELL 25 cm
• RANGE Africa (introduced into other regions)
• HABITAT Forests
• FOOD Plants and decaying matter
The largest land snail has become a pest in some areas and a tasty meal in others. It is also kept as an exotic 'pet', even if it is rather slow with limited behaviour.

Snakelocks sea anemone (p25)
Anemonia, Bolocera (many types)
• SIZE Stalk height and width 5–10 cm, total width up to 30 cm
• SIZE OF TENTACLES Up to 10 cm

- RANGE Temperate seas
- HABITAT Rockpools, shallow water
- FOOD Small fish, prawns, shrimps and similar prey

Anemones look like flowers but they are deadly predators of small seashore creatures. The tentacles are sticky and stinging. They paralyze victims and draw them towards the mouth at their centre.

Giant squid (p17)

Architeuthis harveyi

- SIZE Total length 12 m (including tentacles)
- SIZE OF EYE Up to 40 cm across
- RANGE Oceans worldwide
- HABITAT Deep water
- FOOD Fish, squid and other animals

Because it is so rarely seen, and usually part-decomposed when caught, the giant squid is the subject of many myths. Its eyes however are truly massive, the biggest of any animal, for hunting in deepwater gloom.

Bird-eating spider (p15)

Arvicularia (many kinds)

- SIZE Head and body length up to 10 cm
- SIZE OF FANGS Up to 12 mm
- RANGE Central and South America
- HABITAT Forests, scrub
- FOOD Birds, lizards, mice and similar small animals

The birds consumed by this powerful, hairy spider are usually chicks in the nest that cannot escape. The fangs pierce the victim's body and inject poison and digestive juices that quickly soften its flesh.

Lion's mane jellyfish (p25)

Cyanea (various types)

- SIZE Main body or bell up to 100 cm
- SIZE OF TRAILING TENTACLES Longest are 10 m (or more)
- RANGE Temperate oceans
- HABITAT Open seas
- FOOD Fish, prawns, shrimps and similar prey

This type of jellyfish can be found occurring in many different shapes and sizes. The dozens of outer tentacles are long and fine and can give a painful sting to unwary swimmers.

Medicinal leech (p25)

Hirudo (various types)

- SIZE Length 15 cm (at full stretch)
- SIZE OF SUCKERS Rear one up to 20 mm across, front one smaller
- RANGE Many temperate and warm regions
- HABITAT Ponds, streams, marshes
- FOOD Blood and body fluids

Leeches once sucked blood from people – a medical treatment called blood-letting. Their natural victims are wild horses, asses, deer and cattle. They can move by arching along using front and rear suckers.

North Atlantic lobster (p23)

Homarus americanus

- SIZE Head and body up to 1 m long
- SIZE OF PINCERS Up to 30 cm
- RANGE Atlantic Ocean, especially western shores
- HABITAT Rocky seabed
- FOOD Crabs, shellfish, worms, dead animals

The lobster's bigger claw has rounded lumps for crushing. The smaller one is equipped with sharper ridges for cutting. A big, old, well-fed individual (around 30 years old) could nip off your thumb with either.

Goose barnacle (p33)

Lepas anatifera

- SIZE Stalk and body extend up to 15 cm
- SIZE OF SHELL 5 cm
- RANGE Most warm seas
- HABITAT Fixed to floating logs and similar debris
- FOOD Filters tiny edible particles from the water

The goose barnacle was named because its shell resembles a goose's egg. The barnacle's limbs stick out and look like the emerging feathers of the hatching baby goose.

File shell (p33)

Lima (various types)

- SIZE Up to 12 cm across (including fringe or tentacles)
- SIZE OF SHELL Up to 10 cm
- RANGE Most temperate and tropical seas
- HABITAT Shallow water
- FOOD Filters tiny edible particles from the water

The file shell, a cousin of scallops and clams, cannot shut tight its two shell halves or valves. A gap always remains for the fringe of bright, frilly tentacles that help it to take in oxygen from the water.

Giant (Japanese) spider crab (p23)

Macrocheira kaempferis

- SIZE 30 cm across body, 3 m across outstretched limbs
- SIZE OF PINCERS Up to 20 cm
- RANGE North-west Pacific Ocean
- HABITAT Deep sea bed
- FOOD Scavenges on seabed and catches worms, crabs and other animals

The giant spider crab is adapted to withstand great water pressure at depths of 1,000 m or more. At the surface, with water buoyancy gone, it can hardly move its spindly legs.

Nautilus (p33)

Nautilus pompilius

- SIZE Whole animal 40 cm across
- SIZE OF SHELL 30 cm
- RANGE Pacific Ocean
- HABITAT Mid to deep water
- FOOD Fish, crabs and other prey

The shell is divided inside into chambers. More are added as the nautilus grows, to a maximum of about 30. The nautilus' body occupies the last, largest chamber.

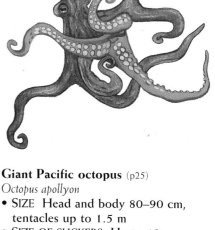

Giant Pacific octopus (p25)

Octopus apollyon

- SIZE Head and body 80–90 cm, tentacles up to 1.5 m
- SIZE OF SUCKERS Up to 10 cm
- RANGE Pacific Ocean
- HABITAT Shallow water to middle depths
- FOOD Fish, crabs, other sea-creatures

The octopus' hard, horny, parrot-like beak and mouth are in the middle of its ring of eight tentacles. The suckered tentacles grab prey and pull it towards the beak, where it is torn to pieces.

Imperial scorpion (p39)

Pandinus imperator

- SIZE Head and body 10 cm
- SIZE OF TAIL 9 cm
- RANGE West Africa
- HABITAT Forests, scrub
- FOOD Grubs, worms, spiders and similar small animals

One of the largest scorpions, the imperial has the typical arched tail with a venomous spine at the tip. It rarely stings its prey but prefers to rip it apart with pincers and jaws, reserving the venom for self-defence.

Glorious starshell (p33)

Pseudastralium henicus

- SIZE Total length 3 cm
- SIZE OF SHELL Main 2 cm, spikes 1 cm
- RANGE West Pacific
- HABITAT Seabed, 100–200 m deep
- FOOD Small animals in the mud

The spiky projections on the shell of this sea snail deter predators from grabbing it as a mouthful. The glorious starshell is an exotic cousin of the common winkles and whelks.

Giant centipede (p23)
Scolopendra gigantea
- SIZE Total length 30 cm (or more)
- SIZE OF PINCER 25 mm
- RANGE Central America, northern South America, Caribbean
- HABITAT Forests, damp scrub, farmland
- FOOD Soil animals such as worms, beetles, grubs, even small mice

A centipede's 'pincers' are really a pair of legs just behind the head that are adapted as venom fangs. They pierce, grip, stab and poison the victim. If molested this centipede will bite back, causing a person great pain.

FISH

Cuttlefish (p35)
Sepia (various types)
- SIZE Head and body 30 cm, eight shortest tentacles 15 cm, longest two tentacles 40 cm
- SIZE OF FIN Width up to 5 cm (around body)
- RANGE Temperate and warmer seas
- HABITAT Mainly shallow seabed
- FOOD Fish, crabs, shrimps, shellfish, worms

The lateral fin forms a flexible fringe all around the body, which the animal waves or undulates to move in any direction. It can also squirt water through its funnel-like siphon for a speedy burst of jet propulsion.

Sturgeon (p29)
Acipenser sturio
- SIZE Total length 3 m
- SIZE OF SCALES Up to 10 cm wide
- RANGE Europe, north-west Asia
- HABITAT Rivers, lakes, shallow seas
- FOOD Bottom-dwelling animals such as worms, crabs, shellfish

The sturgeon is an ancient design of fish left over from prehistoric times. Its scales are big, thick, stiff and bony – compared to the thinner, lighter, much more flexible scales of modern fish.

42

Great white shark (p35)
Carcharodon carcharias
- SIZE Total length 6 m
- SIZE OF DORSAL FIN Height 70 cm
- RANGE Worldwide
- HABITAT Mainly open seas, occasionally coasts
- FOOD Fish, squid, seals, dolphins, whales, carrion

The famous 'Jaws' is the largest predatory shark but, at a reliable average maximum of 6 m, it never seems quite as huge as in the movies. Even so it is powerful, aggressive, voracious and will eat people.

Two-finned flying fish (p27)
Exocetus volitans
- SIZE Length 30 cm
- SIZE OF 'WING' FINS Span 30 cm
- RANGE All warm oceans
- HABITAT Open seas
- FOOD Small fish

The wings of this gliding fish are enlarged pectoral fins. It picks up speed just under the surface with fins folded back, then leaps above and glides for 50 m on a good trip – usually to avoid predators below.

Seahorse (p39)
Hippocampus (various types)
- SIZE Head and body up to 20 cm
- SIZE OF TAIL 10 cm (when straight)
- RANGE Most warm seas
- HABITAT Shallow water, among reefs and seaweed
- FOOD Tiny water animals

The seahorse is a real but unusual fish. It sucks in tiny food through its tube-shaped mouth, clings onto weed or coral with its curly prehensile (grasping) tail, and moves by waving its small dorsal fin.

Sailfish (p35)
Istiophorus platypterus
- SIZE Length 3.5 m
- SIZE OF FIN height 65 cm, length 1.5 m
- RANGE Worldwide in warm seas
- HABITAT Open oceans, rarely inshore
- FOOD Fish and other sea creatures

Just about the fastest fish in the sea, the sailfish thrashes along with its back fin folded flat at up to 100 km/h. Along with the marlin and the swordfish it belongs to the group of powerful predators known as billfish.

Pinecone fish (p29)
Monocentris japonicus
- SIZE Length 12 cm
- SIZE OF SCALES Width up to 1 cm
- RANGE Indian and west Pacific Oceans
- HABITAT Shallow seabeds
- FOOD Small animals such as shrimps, fish, worms

With thick diamond-shaped scales and sharp spines on its back and underside, this is one of the best-protected of all fish. It lives in the twilight zone 100–200 m down and its chin glows an eerie yellow-green.

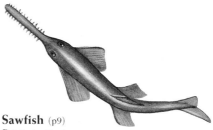

Sawfish (p9)
Pristis pectinata
- SIZE Length 6 m (or more)
- SIZE OF SAW-EDGED SNOUT 2 m
- RANGE Warm seas and oceans worldwide
- HABITAT Shallow coastal waters
- FOOD Bottom-dwelling fish, shellfish, crabs

The amazing snout of this huge fish, a close relative of sharks and rays, is studded with 25–30 saw-like teeth along each side. The fish slices into the mud to disturb, slash and impale prey.

Lionfish (scorpionfish) (p35)
Pterois volitans
- SIZE Total length 40 cm
- SIZE OF FIN SPINES up to 25 cm
- RANGE Indian and Pacific Oceans
- HABITAT Coral reefs, shallow seas
- FOOD Smaller fish, prawns, shellfish and similar animals

The long, sharp, spiny fins of the lionfish are also brightly coloured. They warn enemies: Don't touch! The grooved spines can jab in a powerful poison which has been fatal to humans.

Remora (sharksucker) (p25)
Remora remora
- SIZE Total length 45 cm
- SIZE OF SUCKER DISC 15 cm
- RANGE Worldwide in warm seas
- HABITAT Just underneath its host
- FOOD Small fish, shrimps, also parasites on its host

The remora is one of several hitch-hiking suckerfish that stick to a larger host like a shark, turtle or whale. It receives free rides and sometimes free food too, like scraps from the host's meal or its (other) skin pests.

Red piranha (p15)
Serrasalmus nattereri
- SIZE Total length 30 cm
- SIZE OF TEETH 5–10 mm
- RANGE Amazon region of South America
- HABITAT Rivers, pools
- FOOD Fruits, seeds, small fish, also larger animals when in shoals

The triangular, razor-sharp, blade-like teeth of one piranha can slice out a lump of flesh the size of a hen's egg. When 100 piranhas sense blood from a wounded large animal, their feeding frenzy strips it to a skeleton in minutes.

AMPHIBIANS AND REPTILES

Cane (marine or giant) toad (p19)
Bufo marinus
- SIZE Head and body length 20 cm
- SIZE OF EAR DRUM 17 mm
- RANGE Central and South America, Australia
- HABITAT Forests, scrub, semi-desert, farmland, marshes
- FOOD Any animal it can overpower, even rats

This strong, tough, adaptable toad can cope with drought, flood, fire and even predators. Its body makes a very powerful poison which may kill animals like dogs who attempt to pick it up.

Flap-necked chameleon (p13)
Chameleo dilepsis
- SIZE Total length 30 cm
- SIZE OF TONGUE Up to 12 cm
- RANGE Central and southern Africa
- HABITAT Forests, scrub
- FOOD Small animals such as beetles, spiders, baby birds

The chameleon is green here, for camouflage among leaves. But it can turn almost any colour you may imagine. If confronted by a snake it goes black with yellow spots and hisses loudly!

Goliath frog (p17)
Conraua goliath
- SIZE Head and body length 35 cm (up to 80 cm including legs)
- SIZE OF EYE up to 3 cm
- RANGE West Africa
- HABITAT Rainforests
- FOOD Small animals such as beetles, spiders, worms, mice

The world's largest frog, almost the size of a pet rabbit, is also one of the rarest species of amphibians. Loss of its rainforest home, due to logging and change to farmland, is making it rarer still.

Armadillo lizard (p29)
Cordylus cataphractus
- SIZE Total length 20 cm (or more)
- SIZE OF SCALES 5–10 mm wide
- RANGE Southern Africa
- HABITAT Rocky scrub, semi-desert
- FOOD Worms, insects, spiders

Like its namesake the armadillo (a type of mammal), this lizard rolls into a ball when in danger, tail gripped in its mouth. Or it scuttles off and wedges its flattened body into a crevice among the rocks.

Nile crocodile (p37)
Crocodylus niloticus
- SIZE Total length 5 m
- SIZE OF FOOT Length 30 cm
- RANGE Africa
- HABITAT Rivers, lakes, swamps
- FOOD Animals, from fish and waterfowl to zebra

The croc swims slowly by kicking with its partly-webbed rear feet, using the front feet to steer and brake. For extra speed it folds all four feet against its body and lashes its powerful tail from side to side.

Tokay gecko (p37)
Gekko gekko
- SIZE Total length 25–30 cm
- SIZE OF FEET Toe span 2.5 cm
- RANGE Southern and Southeast Asia
- HABITAT Woods, scrub, also houses and other buildings
- FOOD Cockroaches, spiders, mice, bird chicks and other small animals

With widely-splayed toes, sharp claws and a fringe of gripping velcro-like scales on the underside of the foot, this gecko can easily run up walls and cling on to ceilings. It helpfully eats insect and rodent pests.

Galapagos giant tortoise (p33)
Geochelone (Testudo) elephantus
- SIZE Extended head and body length 1.3 m
- SIZE OF SHELL Up to 1 m long
- RANGE Galapagos Islands, Pacific Ocean
- HABITAT Forests, scrub
- FOOD Leaves and other vegetation

On each island in the Galapagos group, the giant tortoises have their own distinctive shell shape. The tortoise can pull in its head and tail, presenting scaly, well-protected skin to an enemy.

Green tree frog (p31)
Litoria caerulea
- SIZE Total length up to 12 cm
- RANGE North and east Australia, Papua New Guinea
- HABITAT Forests, scrub
- FOOD Flies, bugs, caterpillars and similar small animals

Frogs and toads have poison glands in the skin that ooze horrible-tasting or venomous fluids. The green tree frog is familiar to local people since it rests in flowerpots, drainpipes and even mailboxes.

Alligator snapping turtle (p11)
Macroclemys temmincki
- SIZE Total length up to 65 cm
- SIZE OF MOUTH Width 10 cm
- RANGE Central North America
- HABITAT Rivers, lakes, swamps
- FOOD Fish and similar animals

The 'beak' is formed by sharp edges of tough horn along the line of the jaws. It could easily slice off your finger. Many turtles have this beak-like mouth, since they lack proper cutting teeth.

Indian python (p13)
Python molurus
- SIZE Length up to 6 m
- SIZE OF TONGUE Length 15 cm
- RANGE Southern and Southeast Asia
- HABITAT Forests, swamps, scrub
- FOOD Any animal it can squeeze and swallow

A constrictor, the python coils around prey and squashes its life away. The tongue flicks out to gather airborne scents which are passed to a specialized part in the roof of the mouth, Jacobson's organ, that detects them.

Great crested newt (p35)
Triturus cristatus
- SIZE Total length 15 cm
- SIZE OF BACK FIN OR CREST Height up to 10 mm
- RANGE Europe

- HABITAT Ponds, lakes, slow streams
- FOOD Smaller water animals like worms, tadpoles, baby fish

Also known as the warty newt, only the male has the crinkly, soft crest of skin along the back. This becomes even taller in the breeding season, and his belly turns bright orange.

Gaboon viper (p29)
Vipera gabonica
- SIZE Length 1.5–2 m
- SIZE OF SCALES 8–10 mm
- RANGE West and south-west Africa
- HABITAT Rainforests
- FOOD Mice, rats, frogs, toads, ground birds and similar prey

The wedge-shaped head, narrow neck and brown-green scale pattern make this snake almost impossible to spot among the leaves of the forest floor. It has the longest fangs of any viper, up to 5 cm.

BIRDS

Emperor penguin (p37)
Aptenodytes forsteri
- SIZE Standing height 1.2 m
- SIZE OF FEET Width 12 cm
- RANGE Southern Ocean, Antarctica
- HABITAT Icebergs, pack ice
- FOOD Fish, squid, other sea creatures

The chick hatches from an egg balanced on its father's feet, protected by his thick feathers and a flap of his belly skin. He has stood on the ice like this for nine weeks, never eating. Soon the female returns from feeding at sea to take over, allowing the male to eat at last.

Brown kiwi (p11)
Apteryx australis
- SIZE Total length 50 cm
- SIZE OF BEAK Up to 20 cm
- RANGE New Zealand
- HABITAT Forests
- FOOD Worms, grubs, berries

Kiwis are rare, shy and active only at night, so they are seldom seen in the wild. They have become even more rare as their eggs and chicks are eaten by cats and other predators that have been introduced.

43

Scarlet macaw (p11)
Ara macao
- SIZE Total length 80 cm
- SIZE OF BEAK 10 cm (around curve)
- RANGE Central and South America
- HABITAT Forests, scrub, farmland
- FOOD Seeds, nuts, fruits, berries, other plant food

This colourful and noisy member of the parrot group has suffered greatly in recent years, as its favoured rainforest habitat is felled and wild birds are caught for the pet trade.

Verraux's eagle owl (p17)
Bubo lacteus
- SIZE Total length 65 cm
- SIZE OF EYE 5 cm
- RANGE Africa south of the Sahara
- HABITAT Woodland, scrub, bushy savannah
- FOOD Varied – rats, hares, small monkeys, birds, lizards

This owl's head is smaller than yours – yet its eye is 15-20 mm bigger than ours. The eyeball cannot swivel in its skull socket, so the owl must turn its whole head to look around. Eagle owls often catch smaller owls in mid flight!

Cassowary (p29)
Casuarius casuarias
- SIZE Standing height 1.3 m
- SIZE OF LEG SCALES Width 2.5 cm
- RANGE Indonesia, Papua New Guinea, north-east Australia
- HABITAT Rainforest
- FOOD Fruits, berries, seeds, buds

The cassowary is flightless but far from defenceless since it can kick and slash with its strong legs and huge clawed feet. It lives in the thickest forest, pushing its way through with its head 'helmet' or casque.

White-tipped sicklebill (p11)
Eutoxeres aquila
- SIZE Beak to tail length 14 cm
- SIZE OF BEAK 4 cm
- RANGE Central America and northern South America
- HABITAT Tropical forests

44

- FOOD Nectar

The sicklebill, a type of hummingbird, has the longest and most curved beak for its body size of almost any bird. It probes deep into awkward-shaped flowers such as orchids and heliconias for sugary nectar.

Atlantic puffin (p11)
Fratercula arctica
- SIZE Head to tail length 35 cm
- SIZE OF BEAK 4.5 cm
- RANGE North Atlantic and Arctic Oceans
- HABITAT Coasts
- FOOD Fish, shellfish

Out of the breeding season, the puffin's beak is not only duller in colour, it is smaller because it loses its outer horny sheath. The beak can carry a neat row of up to 20 small fish like sand-eels.

Coot (p37)
Fulica atra
- SIZE Beak to tail length 35 cm
- SIZE OF FOOTPRINT Length up to 15 cm, width up to 12 cm
- RANGE Europe, Asia, Australasia
- HABITAT Lakes, marshes, slow rivers
- FOOD Soft water plants, small water animals

The coot has fleshy lobes along its lengthy toes. These help to spread its weight in soft pondside mud and also give extra push as it kicks its feet to swim and dive after food.

American jacana (lilytrotter) (p21)
Jacana spinosa
- SIZE Beak to tail 25 cm
- SIZE OF CLAW 3 cm (with whole toe nearly 10 cm)
- RANGE Southern North America, Central America
- HABITAT Ponds, lakes, swamps
- FOOD Small water animals, seeds and fruits

The jacana's spidery toes spread its body weight so well that it really can run over floating leaves such as lilies. It pecks at the water's surface for a variety of food and dives in if threatened.

Bee-eater (p27)
Merops apiaster
- SIZE Beak to tail length 30 cm
- SIZE OF WINGS Span 40 cm
- RANGE Europe, Asia, Africa
- HABITAT Woods, shrubland
- FOOD Flying insects

Yes, it really does eat bees, and wasps too. The bee-eater catches them in midair but bashes or rubs them on a branch before swallowing, to damage or remove the sting.

Brown pelican (p11)
Pelecanus occidentalis
- SIZE Head to tail length 1.3 m
- SIZE OF BEAK Up to 50 cm
- RANGE Southern North America, Central America, northern South America, Caribbean
- HABITAT Seashores, islands
- FOOD Fish, squid and similar sea creatures

This is the smallest type of pelican. Unlike its larger relatives, it tends to catch food by plunge-diving from heights of up to 15 m. It curves its neck into an 'S' as it dives.

Greater flamingo (p37)
Phoenicopterus ruber
- SIZE Standing height 1.2 m
- SIZE OF FEET Length up to 15 cm
- RANGE Caribbean, Central America, some Pacific islands
- HABITAT Lakes, coastal lagoons
- FOOD Tiny water creatures like shrimps, worms and shellfish

The flamingo is one of the tallest – and pinkest – wading birds. Its strong, scaly, long-toed feet are ideal for spreading its weight over soft mud and sand.

Ostrich (egg) (p33)
Struthio camelus
- SIZE About 16 x 14 cm
- VOLUME Equivalent to 40 average hen's eggs
- RANGE Africa, Middle East
- HABITAT Grassland, scrub, desert
- FOOD Adults eat almost anything

From the largest egg of any living bird, the ostrich chick hatches out and grows into the largest of any adult bird, standing up to 2.5 m tall. It is also the fastest-running bird at up to 70 km/h.

Barn owl (p21)
Tyto alba
- SIZE Head to tail length 35 cm
- SIZE OF TALONS 2 cm
- RANGE Most of the world
- HABITAT Woods, fields, bush, shrubland
- FOOD Mice, voles and similar small animals

Easily the world's most widespread owl, this usually ghost-white bird grips and stabs its prey to death with its powerful, sharp talons. It can also impale small birds caught in a flypast from a branch or on the wing.

Andean condor (p27)
Vultur gryphus
- SIZE Beak to tail length 1.2 m
- SIZE OF WINGS Span 2.5 m
- RANGE Andes Mountains, hills of South America
- HABITAT Rocky, remote uplands
- FOOD Carrion (dead or dying animals)

No other bird has a larger wing area than the Andean condor, although the wandering albatross has a greater wingspan. This immense vulture can soar for 10 km without flapping and spot food from this distance too.

PLANT-EATING MAMMALS

Black spider monkey (p39)
Ateles paniscus
- SIZE Head and body length 50 cm
- SIZE OF TAIL Length 70 cm
- RANGE Northern South America
- HABITAT Forests
- FOOD Fruits, nuts, seeds, leaves

Owner of one of most prehensile (grasping) tails in the animal kingdom, the black spider monkey can easily hang from it or pick fruit with it. Near the tip on the underside is a bare patch with skin ridges, like our own fingertips, for extra grip.

Three-toed sloth (p21)
Bradypus tridactylus
- SIZE Head and body length 60 cm
- SIZE OF CLAW 10 cm around curve
- RANGE Central and South America
- HABITAT Forests
- FOOD Leaves, buds, fruits and other plant material

The sloth's whole lifestyle is in the slow lane. It chews lazily, moves hardly faster than a snail, and produces droppings just once a week. The massive curved claws hook it on to branches, day in, day out.

Dromedary camel (p37)
Camelus dromedarius
- SIZE Head and body length 3 m, tail length 50 cm
- SIZE OF FOOT Width 25 cm
- RANGE Africa, Middle East, Australia
- HABITAT Grasslands, dry scrub, deserts
- FOOD Grasses and other plants

The one-humped camel has wide, soft feet with splayed toes and small hooves. They are designed both to stop it sinking in soft sand and to grip slippery rocks. A thirsty camel drinks 100 litres of water in a few minutes.

American beaver (p39)
Castor canadensis
- SIZE Head and body length 90 cm
- SIZE OF TAIL Length 25 cm
- RANGE North America
- HABITAT Lakes, rivers, creeks in woodland
- FOOD Trees – bark, twigs, buds, leaves, roots

The beaver's scaly-looking tail is covered by short ridges of the usual leathery mammal skin. Its main job is to be slapped down onto the water's surface with a loud splash to warn the rest of the family if danger is near.

White (square-lipped) rhinoceros (p31)
Ceratotherium simum
- SIZE Head and body length 5 m
- SIZE OF SKIN Up to 3 cm thick
- RANGE Central and southern Africa
- HABITAT Grassland
- FOOD Grass

The body of the rhino has few hairs except for around the eyes, nostrils, ear-tips and tail. However the nose horn is almost solid hairs. They grow compressed and cemented together, almost as hard as bone.

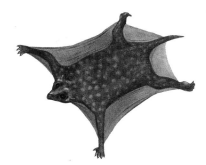

Colugo (flying lemur) (p27)
Cynocephalus variegatus
- SIZE Head and body 40 cm, tail 25 cm
- SIZE OF 'WINGS' Span 70 cm
- RANGE Southeast Asia
- HABITAT Forests
- FOOD Leaves, buds, flowers, soft fruits

Neither a flier nor a lemur, the colugo is a gliding relation of shrews and moles. It is the most expert of parachuting mammals, regularly swooping distances of more than 100 m on its thin skin panels yet losing only 10 m in height.

Asian elephant (p9)
Elephas maximus
- SIZE Head and body length 6 m (excludes trunk and tail)
- SIZE OF TRUNK Length 1.5–2 m
- RANGE South and east Asia, from India to China and Indonesia
- HABITAT Forests and scrubby grassland
- FOOD Leaves, grasses, shoots, fruits, bark

An elephant's trunk is its very long, joined-together nose and upper lip. It's used for smelling, feeling, stroking friends, trumpeting, grasping, putting in the mouth, sucking up water or sand to squirt out – and of course breathing.

Grevy's zebra (p19)
Equus grevyi
- SIZE Head and body 2.7 m, tail 60 cm
- SIZE OF EAR Height 25 cm
- RANGE North-east and east Africa
- HABITAT Grassland, dry scrub
- FOOD Grasses and other plant parts

Largest of the three types of zebra, Grevy's has the tallest ears and most erect mane. The ears constantly swivel to the front, sides and rear to scan for interesting sounds. They come forward to listen intently. If they go flat back, beware – it's a bite or kick!

Giraffe (p31)
Giraffa camelopardalis
- SIZE Height to horn tips (male) 5.5 m
- SIZE OF HAIRS Length 3–5 cm (on most of body)
- RANGE Africa, south of the Sahara
- HABITAT Grassland, bush, open woods
- FOOD Leaves, shoots and fruits

The coat pattern of a giraffe is almost as individual as our fingerprints. Some individuals have light yellow patches, others almost black. The white background may be just thin lines or thicker than the patches.

Long-tongued bat (p13)
Glossophaga soricina
- SIZE Head and body length 6 cm
- SIZE OF TONGUE 3 cm
- RANGE Central and South America, Caribbean
- HABITAT Woods and dry scrub
- FOOD Nectar and pollen

Most bats eat flying insects such as moths. But this type is like a night-time hummingbird. It hovers at flowers and licks the pollen and nectar from deep within using its long, bristle-tipped tongue.

Naked mole rat (p31)
Heterocephalus glaber
- SIZE Head and body length 9 cm, tail length 3 cm
- SIZE OF HAIRS Length up to 2 cm (but very sparse)
- RANGE East Africa
- HABITAT Dry sandy scrub, grassland
- FOOD Roots, bulbs and other underground plant parts

One of the strangest mammals, the naked mole-rat lives in tunnels like a mole. It is a group-dweller and only a single female, the queen, can breed at any time. If she dies a 'worker' matures and takes her place.

Ring-tailed lemur (p39)
Lemur catta
- SIZE Head and body length 45 cm
- SIZE OF TAIL Length 55 cm
- RANGE Madagascar
- HABITAT Open woodland and scrub
- FOOD Plant material such as leaves, fruits, sap

The lemur's tail is a 'smelly striped flag'. The owner wipes it over scent glands on its arms and genital region, then holds it erect. It can be seen clearly and the personal scent can waft past the rest of the troop.

Black-tailed jackrabbit (p19)
Lepus californicus
- SIZE Head and body length 60 cm
- SIZE OF EAR Length 20 cm
- RANGE Central North America
- HABITAT Prairie, farmland, dry scrub
- FOOD Seeds, grass and other plant parts

In addition to catching the slightest sound, this hare's huge ears also give off excess body heat during the sweltering summer. They angle back as the jackrabbit dashes along with speedy leaps at nearly 60 km/h.

African elephant (p19)
Loxodonta africanus
- SIZE Head and body length 7 m (excludes trunk and tail)
- SIZE OF EAR Up to 1.5 m wide
- RANGE Africa
- HABITAT Forests, bush, grassland
- FOOD Grass, leaves and other plants

Famous for flapping its ears to keep cool, the elephant uses many sounds to communicate with its herd. Some calls are so rumbling and deep (infrasonic) that we cannot hear them – our ear flaps are far too small to catch the long sound waves.

Proboscis monkey (p9)
Nasalis larvatus
- SIZE Head and body length 65 cm, tail length 65 cm
- SIZE OF NOSE 6 cm
- RANGE Borneo in Southeast Asia
- HABITAT Mangrove forests, riverbanks, swamps
- FOOD Leaves and fruits

46

The proboscis monkey is the most specialized plant-eater of all monkeys. The male is bigger than the female and has a much longer, more dangling nose. It goes straight and rigid as he honks his mating call.

Okapi (p13)
Okapia johnstoni
- SIZE Head and body length 2 m
- SIZE OF TONGUE Length 30 cm
- RANGE West Africa
- HABITAT Dense rainforests
- FOOD Leaves, shoots, fruits and other plant food

The okapi's tongue is so lengthy that it can clean out its own ears by licking them. This shy and rare animal lives alone and, like its close cousin, the giraffe, only the male animal has the short horns.

Koala (p9)
Phascolarctos cinereus
- SIZE Head and body length 70 cm
- SIZE OF NOSE 10 cm (top to bottom)
- RANGE East Australia
- HABITAT Eucalypt woodland
- FOOD Leaves, mainly eucalypts and similar gums

The koala, a marsupial or pouched mammal, may look cute and cuddly. But it can scratch fiercely with its long, sharp claws. Koalas live in their food trees, only coming down to the ground to ascend another one.

MEAT-EATING MAMMALS

Star-nosed mole (p9)
Condylura cristata
- SIZE Head and body 12 cm, tail 7 cm
- SIZE OF NOSE 2.5 cm across
- RANGE Eastern North America
- HABITAT Damp soil with ponds and streams

- FOOD Small water creatures such as fish, worms, shellfish, insects

The star-nosed mole lives in a tunnel system, like other moles, but does not find its food there. Instead, this expert swimmer dives and feels with its nose frill of 22 tentacles for swimming or wriggling food.

Aye-aye (p21)
Daubentonia madagascariensis
- SIZE Head and body length 40 cm, tail length 50 cm
- SIZE OF MIDDLE FINGER Length 12–15 cm
- RANGE North and east Madagascar
- HABITAT Dense forests
- FOOD Grubs and other small animals, fruits, eggs

One of the world's rarest and most specialized animals, the aye-aye is a cousin of the lemurs. It hunts through trees at night, poking and picking out grubs from bark with its extraordinary long middle fingers.

Lesser bushbaby (p17)
Galago senegalis
- SIZE Head and body 17 cm, tail 23 cm
- SIZE OF EYE 2 cm
- RANGE Most of central and southern Africa
- HABITAT Woods, scrub, bush (not dense rainforests)
- FOOD Very varied including small tree animals like beetles, spiders, lizards and birds, also fruits, flowers, shoots, buds, nectar

It's just as well the bushbaby sees so clearly, since it bounces around the treetops at night like a spring-loaded toy. Its huge forward-facing eyes give binocular (stereoscopic) vision to judge distances accurately.

Sun bear (p21)
Helarctos malayanus
- SIZE Head and body length 1.3 m
- SIZE OF CLAWS Length 5–7 cm
- RANGE Southeast Asia

- HABITAT Forests
- FOOD Wide variety of small animals, also fruits, nuts and leaves

The sun bear is the smallest and most tree-living of the seven kinds of bear, with long, sharp claws to grip branches. It rips off bark to get at wood-boring grubs, beetles, wild bee honey and other snacks.

Giant pangolin (p29)
Manis gigantea
- SIZE Head and body 80 cm, tail 60 cm
- SIZE OF SCALES Width up to 5 cm (across the largest)
- RANGE West and south-west Africa
- HABITAT Forests, bush
- FOOD Ants, termites

This 'pinecone' version of an anteater has an almost all-over covering of thick, sharp-edged scales. When it rolls into a ball wrapped within its own tail, even a lion or leopard cannot break in.

Narwhal (p15)
Monodon monoceros
- SIZE Total length 6 m
- SIZE OF TUSK Up to 2.6 m
- RANGE Arctic Ocean
- HABITAT Open seas
- FOOD Fish, squid, shrimps, crabs

Only the male has the amazing spiralled tusk, which is actually an overgrown tooth – the upper left incisor. (Some older females have much shorter versions.) At breeding time males 'fence' using them like swords.

Giant anteater (p13)
Myrmecophaga tridactyla
- SIZE Head and body 1.2 m, tail 90 cm
- SIZE OF TONGUE Up to 60 cm
- RANGE Central and South America
- HABITAT Woods, scrub, grassland
- FOOD Ants, termites

After ripping a hole in the side of the nest, the anteater flicks out its tongue 2–3 times each second for about one minute, gathering 200–300 ants as prey. Then it moves on, leaving the nest for repair and a future snack.

Slit-faced bat (p19)
Nycterus (various types)
- SIZE Head and body length 12 cm
- SIZE OF EAR 4 cm
- RANGE Africa, Asia
- HABITAT Forests, bush
- FOOD Small animals including moths, beetles, spiders, scorpions

Slit-faced bats are named from skin grooves running from the nose-tip upwards and towards each eye. They swoop with great agility to catch small prey on branches, tree trunks and even on the ground.

Walrus (p15)
Odobenus rosmarus
- SIZE Total length 3 m
- SIZE OF TUSK 60 cm
- RANGE Arctic Ocean
- HABITAT Islands, icebergs
- FOOD Bottom-dwelling shellfish, crabs and worms

Walrus-watchers identify individuals by tusk length and angle. Each tusk is a very large upper canine tooth. It's a chisel to chip shellfish from the seabed, and a pick as the walrus hauls itself out on to the ice.

Killer whale (orca) (p35)
Orcinus orca
- SIZE Length 9 m (male)
- SIZE OF FIN Height 2 m (male)
- RANGE All seas and oceans
- HABITAT Mainly coastal waters
- FOOD Anything it fancies – mainly fish, dolphins and small whales

The male killer's fin is tall and triangular, the female's is shorter and more curved (crescent). The largest type of dolphin, it co-operates with others in its pod (group) to catch all kinds of prey, from fish to great whales.

Platypus (p11)
Ornithorhynchus anatinus
- SIZE Total length 60 cm
- SIZE OF BILL 10 cm
- RANGE Eastern Australia
- HABITAT Lakes, rivers, creeks
- FOOD Aquatic worms, insects, small shellfish, fish and frogs

The platypus is one of only three types of egg-laying mammals, or monotremes. Its extraordinary 'duck bill' senses delicate touches and also weak electrical signals in the water made by the moving muscles of its prey.

Aardvark (p9)
Orycteropus afer
- SIZE Head and body length 1.5 m, tail length 50 cm
- LENGTH OF SNOUT 20 cm
- RANGE Africa, south of the Sahara
- HABITAT Varied – from dense forests to semi-desert
- FOOD Termites and ants

The secretive 'earth pig' lives alone and is active at night. It sniffs out tiny prey with its very sensitive nostrils, rips open the nest with its strongly-clawed forefeet and finally licks up the meal with its sticky tongue.

Lion (p15)
Panthera leo
- SIZE Head and body 2 m, tail 1 m
- SIZE OF LARGEST TOOTH (CANINE) 8 cm
- RANGE Central and southern Africa, north-west India
- HABITAT Grassland and scrub
- FOOD Medium and large animals

The dagger-like canine teeth stab and rip big prey so it quickly bleeds to death. Or the lion may clamp its jaws onto the windpipe of a smaller victim so that it suffocates. The small incisor teeth at the front of the mouth nip and nibble meat from bone.

Black panther (leopard) (p31)
Panthera pardus
- SIZE Head and body 1.6 m, tail 1 m
- SIZE OF SPOTS 2–10 cm
- RANGE Africa and southern Asia
- HABITAT Almost anywhere, from mountains to farmland and semi-desert
- FOOD Almost any prey, from mice to young elephants

Amazingly adaptable, the leopard cannot change its spots. Even the black or melanic form, commonly called the black panther, shows the typical leopard pattern – actually groups of spots like rose petals.

Bengal tiger (p17)
Panthera tigris
- SIZE Head and body 2 m, tail up to 1 m
- SIZE OF EYE 3.5 cm
- RANGE Southern Asia
- HABITAT Forests, scrub, swamps
- FOOD Medium and large mammals

The tiger hunts alone mainly at dawn or dusk. It picks up a scent trail, then uses its keen sight for the stealthy approach and the final full-power charge of 15–20 m. Even so, only one attempt in about 12 is successful.

Humpback dolphin (p39)
Sousa chinensis
- SIZE Total length 2.2 m
- SIZE OF TAIL Width 60 cm
- RANGE Indian and west Pacific Oceans
- HABITAT Coasts, estuaries
- FOOD Fish, squid, shellfish, crabs and other water creatures

This small dolphin lives in groups of about 20 which sometimes swim up rivers, especially the Ch'ang-jiang (in China) into swampland. They find their way in the muddy water by

squeaks and clicks of sound-radar (echolocation), like bats.

European mole (p21)
Talpa europaea
- SIZE Head and body 14 cm, tail 4 cm
- SIZE OF FORELIMB CLAWS 8–10 mm
- RANGE Europe, Western Asia
- HABITAT Woods, scrub, grassland
- FOOD Worms, slugs, grubs and similar soil animals

In soft soil a mole can dig 20 m of tunnel in one day, using its powerful forelimbs with their wide, thick, long claws like shovels. It patrols the tunnels regularly and eats creatures that fall into them.

Bottle-nosed dolphin (p15)
Tursiops truncatus
- SIZE Total length 4 m
- SIZE OF TEETH Length up to 12 mm
- RANGE Temperate and warm oceans
- HABITAT Coastal waters
- FOOD Squid, fish, shellfish, seabirds

A dolphin's numerous (around 120) but small, slightly blunt, cone-shaped teeth may not look especially fearsome. But they are the ideal design for grasping slimy, slippery, wriggling prey.

Fennec fox (p19)
Vulpes zerda
- SIZE Head and body length 40 cm
- SIZE OF EAR Length 15 cm
- RANGE Northern and central Africa, Middle East
- HABITAT Deserts, dry scrub
- FOOD Mice, small birds, lizards, insects, eggs

The fennec fox sleeps by day in its burrow to avoid the desert heat. By night it hunts as much by sound as by sight and scent, even hearing the sand grains pushed aside by a small running beetle.

Index